THE BEST DOGS EVER

GREAT DANES ARE THE BEST!

Elaine Landau

LERNER PUBLICATIONS COMPANY · MINNEAPOLIS

For Daniel Nkansha

Lerner Publications Company
A division of Lerner Publishing Group, Inc.
241 First Avenue North
Minneapolis, MN 55401 U.S.A.

Website address: www.lernerbooks.com

Library of Congress Cataloging-in-Publication Data

Landau, Elaine.
     Great Danes are the best! / by Elaine Landau.
        p.   cm. — (The best dogs ever)
     Includes index.
     ISBN 978-0-7613-6079-7 (lib. bdg. : alk. paper)
     1. Great Dane—Juvenile literature. I. Title.
  SF429.G7L357 2011
  636.73–dc22   2010022525

Manufactured in the United States of America
1 — CG — 12/31/10

TABLE OF CONTENTS

CHAPTER ONE

A HUGE POOCH

Do you think big is beautiful? Do you like really large dogs? How about one the size of a small pony? If this sounds like you, then I have a pooch I'd like you to meet. It's the Great Dane!

Great Danes are one of the world's largest dog breeds.

A Great Dane is a strong, powerful canine. These dogs have square, muscular bodies. They are well formed and graceful. Anyone would be proud to be seen with a Great Dane.

THE BEST NAME FOR THE BEST WOOFER

Great Danes are special dogs. Every special dog should have a special name. Do any of these fit your wonderful woofer?

Goliath

Highness

Legend

Longfellow

Athena

ZEUS

Dazzler

Atlantis

Omega

Just How Big Are They?

Most male Great Danes are at least 32 inches (81 centimeters) tall at the shoulder. Yet these dogs can be even bigger. Some males are more than 38 inches (97 cm) tall at the shoulder and weigh nearly 200 pounds (91 kilograms). Female Great Danes are a little smaller.

A Great Dane (*above*) is much larger than a Chihuahua (*right*).

Handsome and Colorful

Great Danes aren't just big. They're good looking too. They don't all look alike either. Great Danes come in these great colors and patterns.

- black
- blue (a grayish color)
- fawn (golden beige)
- brindle (brown with black stripes)
- harlequin (white with black patches)
- mantle (mostly black with white areas on the muzzle, chest, legs, and tail tip)

Great Danes can be many colors, including blue *(above)* and black *(top)*.

The Best about the Breed

Don't let their size fool you. Great Danes are really sweet and gentle. They are sometimes even called gentle giants.

This boy cuddles up next to his Great Dane.

Great Danes are quiet, loving dogs. They enjoy being around their human family. They are happiest at their owners' sides. Their owners think they have the best dogs ever. Wouldn't you agree?

Scooby-Doo (below) is a popular Great Dane from a TV show. The cartoon dog has also starred in movies.

SCOOBY-DOO — ONE FAMOUS GREAT DANE

Have you ever watched Scooby-Doo? This show stars a cartoon dog who solves mysteries with his four teenage friends. They drive around in a van called the Mystery Machine. What's the best thing about Scooby-Doo? He's a Great Dane!

CHAPTER TWO

THE HISTORY OF A GREAT DOG

True or False?

The Great Dane is a Danish dog. It comes from Denmark.

The answer is false. Are you surprised? You might think this dog's from Denmark because of its name. But the Great Dane comes from Germany.

A woman pets her Great Dane in this image from an 1800s German magazine.

A German animal trainer and circus owner poses with his Great Dane in the early 1900s.

Hardworking Dogs

In Germany, Great Danes were working dogs. They were used to hunt wild boars (hogs) in the country's thick forests. Later, Great Danes were also used as guard dogs.

Three Great Danes stand alert on a hilltop.

Those early Great Danes were not like the dogs
we know in modern times. They were bred to
hunt and were much fiercer. The dogs did their
job well, but they were not family pets.

These Great Danes
work outside in 1803.

A LONG HISTORY

The Great Dane is not a new breed. It's been around for at least four hundred years. In the mid-1600s, German noblemen kept these dogs on their estates (large areas of land with houses on them). They wanted the largest, fiercest dogs for hunting and guarding.

This scene (*below*) from *Marmaduke* shows the film's star getting a bath.

Children (*above*) rest with their Great Dane pet in 1959.

Creating a Cuddly Canine

In the late 1800s, breeders decided to change things. They hoped to create a kinder, gentler Great Dane. Over time, they did this through careful breeding. The new and improved Great Dane was handsome, huggable, and easygoing. It would be hard to find a finer pet!

MAKE WAY FOR MARMADUKE!

Marmaduke is a lovable dog from a comic strip. He's also a Great Dane. Marmaduke has really long legs and a big, toothy grin. He's got lots of spunk to boot.

Marmaduke is one popular pooch. His comic strip appears in more than six hundred newspapers. This dog has about 45 million fans in twenty countries! Marmaduke even made it to the big screen in his own feature flick. In this movie, the pony-sized pooch has lots of new fun adventures.

The Working Group

The American Kennel Club (AKC) groups dogs by breed. Some of the AKC's groups include the toy group, the hound group, and the herding group. Great Danes are in the working group.

Basset hounds, like this one, are in the hound group.

Border collies belong to the herding group.

Yorkshire terriers, like this one, are in the toy group.

Dogs in the working group tend to be large, strong, and smart. At times, these dogs have been used as guard dogs and hunters. Some have pulled sleds or done rescue work.

This working-group dog guards a family's home.

A Newfoundland is a working-group dog that performs water rescue work.

CHAPTER THREE

THE RIGHT CHOICE FOR YOU?

You love giant dogs. You long for a huge, powerful pooch. Your heart is set on a Great Dane.

One of the world's tallest dogs stands next to his loving owner.

But is bigger always better? Is a Great Dane really the perfect pooch for you? Read on to find out.

Great Danes are wonderful dogs— but they aren't right for everyone.

Got Space at Your Place?

A full-grown Great Dane will weigh more than you. What if it stretches out on the couch? Don't count on sitting there too. There won't be room. Big dogs often do best in big houses. A large, fenced-in yard doesn't hurt either. If you live in a small apartment, think about getting another breed.

A Great Dane can take up a lot of space on your bed or couch.

How's Your Get Up and Go?

Great Danes need exercise to stay healthy. Two to three short walks a day will do.

Are you a couch potato? Did you plan on only walking your dog to the nearest tree? If so, you might be better off with a hamster or a cat.

Great Danes love to exercise.

An Indoor Dog

Great Danes are indoor dogs. Don't try leaving a Great Dane outside in a yard all day. You'll have one unhappy canine. Great Danes like being around humans. Your dog will want your company.

A Great Dane enjoys spending time with his owners over the holidays.

A High-Priced Pooch

Great Danes are purebred dogs. Their puppies can be pretty pricey. A full-grown Great Dane needs lots of food as well. Are you sure you can afford a pricey pet? Talk this over with your family.

RESCUE A GREAT DANE

Can't afford a Great Dane puppy? How about getting an older dog? You can find terrific older dogs at Great Dane rescue centers. Often you can get one for a low fee. Just remember: All dogs are expensive. Even if you don't pay much for your new pet, you will still need to spend money on toys, health care, treats, and more. But adopting a rescued dog can help you cut down on the purchase price.

Have you decided if a Great Dane is your kind of dog? If it is, you're in for a treat. A super dog is about to come your way. Get set for tons of fun!

ALL IN THE FAMILY

Great Danes enjoy being part of family events and outings. These dogs do well with both kids and older people. And they usually get along with other household pets.

CHAPTER FOUR
WELCOME YOUR WOOFER

What a terrific day! You're getting your Great Dane. You've waited a long time for this. You want everything to be perfect.

Be Ready

Help things go smoothly by having the basics ready for your dog. Not sure what you'll need to welcome Fido to your family? Try starting off with these items.

- collar
- leash
- tags (for identification)
- dog food
- food and water bowls
- crates (one for when your pet travels by car and one for it to rest in at home)
- treats (to be used in training)
- toys

Time to See the Veterinarian

Take your dog to a veterinarian as soon as possible. That's a doctor who takes care of animals. They are called vets for short. The vet will check your dog's health. Your dog will also get its shots. Take your dog back to the vet for regular checkups. Also take your dog to the vet if it gets sick.

A veterinarian makes sure this Great Dane is healthy.

Feeding Your Huge Pooch

Ask your vet what to feed your pet.
Dogs need different foods at
different times in their lives. Keep
your dog on a healthful diet.
Don't feed it table scraps.

A Great Dane
eats dog food
from a dish.

TRAINING IS A MUST

Start training your Great Dane early. Though gentle, these huge dogs are very powerful. They can easily knock over a child without meaning to. But there's also some good news. Great Danes are smart and easy to train. They want to please their owners.

Clipping your dog's nails is a part of grooming.

Gotta Groom That Pooch

Lucky you! Great Danes are short-haired dogs. Their coats don't matt or tangle. Just brush your dog daily to keep its coat clean and shiny.

KEEP THINGS CALM

Want all your friends to see your new dog? Don't worry. They'll meet your furry pal soon enough. Just don't have lots of guests over on your dog's first day home. Give your pet a chance to get used to its new house and family.

You and Your Great Dane

Great Danes are great dogs. Your dog will be your best friend. Be its best friend as well.

Give your dog the time and attention it deserves. Be the kind of owner your dog would be proud of. And you'll feel proud of yourself too.

Glossary

American Kennel Club (AKC): an organization that groups dogs by breed. The AKC also defines the characteristics of different breeds.

breed: a particular type of dog. Dogs of the same breed have the same body shape and general features. *Breed* can also refer to producing puppies.

breeder: someone who mates dogs to produce a particular type of dog

brindle: brown with black stripes

canine: a dog, or having to do with dogs

coat: a dog's fur

diet: the food your dog eats

harlequin: white with black patches

mantle: mostly black with white areas on the muzzle, chest, legs, and tail tip

matt: to become severely tangled. Matting causes fur to clump together in large masses.

muzzle: a dog's nose, mouth, and jaws

purebred: a dog whose parents are of the same breed

rescue center: a shelter where stray and abandoned dogs are kept until they are adopted

veterinarian: a doctor who treats animals. Veterinarians are called vets for short.

working group: a group of dogs that were bred to do different types of jobs, such as guarding property, carrying messages, or pulling sleds

FOR MORE INFORMATION

Books

Brecke, Nicole, and Patricia M. Stockland. *Dogs You Can Draw*. Minneapolis: Millbrook Press, 2010. Perfect for dog lovers, this colorful book teaches readers how to draw many different popular dog breeds.

Fiedler, Julie. *Great Danes*. New York: PowerKids Press, 2006. This book explores the history of the Great Dane as well as its role as a family pet.

Landau, Elaine. *Your Pet Dog*. Rev. ed. New York: Children's Press, 2007. This title is a good guide for young people on choosing and caring for a dog.

Markle, Sandra. *Animal Heroes: True Rescue Stories*. Minneapolis: Millbrook Press, 2009. Markle tells how dogs and other animals have helped humans in dangerous situations.

Murray, Julie. *Great Danes*. Edina, MN: Abdo, 2003. This text offers a look at the characteristics of Great Danes and provides tips on caring for these dogs.

Websites

American Kennel Club
http://www.akc.org
Visit this website to find a complete listing of AKC-registered dog breeds, including the Great Dane. The site also features fun printable activities for kids.

ASPCA Kids
http://www.aspca.org/aspcakids/pet-care
Check out this page for helpful hints on caring for a dog and other pets.

LERNER *e* SOURCE

Expand learning beyond the printed book. Download free, complementary educational resources for this book from our website, www.lerneresource.com

Index

Photo Acknowledgments

The images in this book are used with the permission of: backgrounds © iStockphoto.com/Julie Fisher and © iStockphoto.com/Tomasz Adamczyk; © iStockphoto.com/Michael Balderas, p. 1; © Bruce Coleman/Photoshot, p. 4; © Radius Images/Photolibrary, p. 5 (left); © Michael Blann/Stone/Getty Images, p. 5 (right); AP Photo/Science, Deanne Fitzmaurice, p. 6; © Imagesource/Photolibrary, p. 7 (top); © iStockphoto.com/Michelle Harvey, p. 7 (bottom); © Mel Yates/Taxi/Getty Images, p. 8; © Jupiterimages/ Photolibrary, p. 9 (top); Warner Brothers/The Kobal Collection, p. 9 (bottom); © Pauline St Dennis/CORBIS, p. 10 (left); © Studio 504/Photodisc/Getty Images, p. 10 (right); © INTERFOTO/Alamy, p. 11 (both); © Mary Evans Picture Library/The Image Works, pp. 12 (both), 13; © William Gottlieb /CORBIS, p. 14 (top); Twentieth Century Fox Film Corporation/The Kobal Collection, p. 14 (bottom); © Jerry Shulman/SuperStock, p. 15 (basset hound); © Nataliya Kuznetsova | Dreamstime.com , p. 15 (yorkie); © Eric Isselée/Shutterstock Images, p. 15 (border collie); © H. Arnstrong Roberts/Retrofile/Getty Images, p. 16 (top); © Jean-Luc & Francoise Ziegler/Photolibrary, p. 16 (bottom); © Deanne Fitzmaurice/CORBIS, p. 17; © Siri Stafford/Getty Images, p. 18; © Erin Vey/Flickr/Getty Images, p. 19 (top); © Eri Morita/Digital Vision/Getty Images, p. 19 (bottom); © Matt Gray/Digital Vision/Getty Images, p. 20; © Brian Summers/CORBIS, p. 21 (top); © Syracuse Newspapers/The Image Works, p. 21 (bottom); © Martin Harvey/Digital Vision/Getty Images, p. 22 (top); © iStockphoto.com/ Denny Medley, p. 22 (bottom); © Brand X Pictures/Getty Images, p. 23 (bottom); © 2UPPA /Topham/The Image Works, p. 23 (top); © Yellow Dog Productions/Stone/ Getty Images, p. 24; © iStockphoto.com/orix3, p. 25 (yellow dog toy); © Tootles/Dreamstime.com, p. 25 (red dog collar); © Uturnpix/Dreamstime.com, p. 25 (dog dishes and leash); © Sanclemenesdigpro/Dreamstime.com, p. 25 (right); © iStockphoto.com/Chris Bernard, p. 26; © Marta Johnson, pp. 27 (top), 28 (bottom); © Tierfotoagentur/Alamy, p. 27 (bottom); © Martin Harvey/Photolibrary, p. 28; © Mark Raycroft/Minden Pictures, p. 29.

Front Cover: © Mark Raycroft/Minden Pictures
Back Cover: © Eric Isselée/Dreamstime.com